JESSIE PAEGE

HEY, it's okay to be <u>you</u>

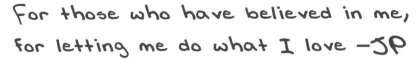

For those who have believed in me,
for letting me do what I love —JP

SIZZLE
PRESS

An imprint of Bonnier Publishing USA
251 Park Avenue South, New York, NY 10010
Copyright © 2017 by Jessie Paege
Text by Sheila Sweeny Higginson
Illustrations by Steph Stilwell
Cover and additional photography on pages 3, 5, 6, 16, and 107 by Jon Sams.
Manufactured in The United States of America VEP 1017
First Edition
10 9 8 7 6 5 4 3 2 1
ISBN 978-1-4998-0704-2
sizzlepressbooks.com
bonnierpublishingusa.com

Hello, my people!

I'm Jessie Paege. I have my own YouTube channel where I talk about self-confidence, fashion, and life. I've shared a lot with my fans through my videos, including my experiences being bullied and living with anxiety. Posting my thoughts and hearing from fans has brought me to a better place in life. I want that for you too.

So, I created this book for you. It's something to hold in your hands, something we can share, and something to lead you to a better place. Think of this as our shared personal journal. I've included my thoughts, feelings, my worries—you do the same. Fill in every spare inch of this book and reveal the truest, original YOU!

 Jessie

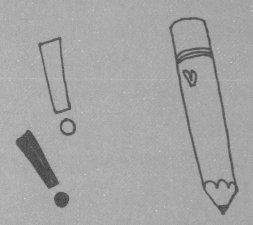

Okay, now let me get to know you.

THIS BOOK BELONGS TO _____

ACTUAL AGE _____

MENTAL AGE _____

DREAM HAIR COLOR _____

FANDOMS _____

FAVORITE MUSIC _____

PET PEEVE _____

A DISNEY PRINCESS WHO SHOULD EXIST _____

_____

A MOVIE PLOT LINE THAT NEEDS TO HAPPEN _____

_____

OTHER YOUTUBERS I WATCH _____

_____

TWO TV SHOWS THAT SHOULD CROSS OVER _____

_____

IF YOU FIND THIS BOOK, PLEASE . . . _____

_____

CODE OF CONDUCT

Here are the rules. It's like the first day of school, when you learn what you need to do for the rest of the year, but only not as lame. I mean, I'm the teacher here...so promise me you'll:

- Accept that you might get emotional. There are some serious issues to think about in here, and you're going to have to be honest and open.
- Tap into the power of positivity. Give yourself something beautiful to look back on in 10 years.
- Get brutal. Look closely at the tough stuff you try to ignore. You never have to show this book to anyone—it's personal.
- Read closely and get thoughtful. Apply the lessons in this book to your own world.
- Ditch fake personas. Your true self is not just welcome here, it's required.

ME, CURRENTLY

People change rapidly. I look, think, and express myself very differently than I did 10 years ago. Who knows what you'll be like by the time you finish this book? These pages are for you to look back at and reflect upon.

FEELING creative and passionate

LOVING going to the movies by myself

INSPIRED BY my audience, other pals I meet from YouTube

DESPERATELY SEEKING a better balance in my life

Paste or draw yourself here and fill in the blanks. Add to the doodles!

FEELING _____

LOVING _____

INSPIRED BY _____

_____

DESPERATELY SEEKING _____

_____

IT'S OKAY TO...

DISCONNECT

Obsessed with social media? Me too. Social media can help you build online communities, but it can also keep you from connecting with the people in the room.

ADVICE ON DISCONNECTING

- Try hobbies and activities that don't involve your phone.
- Social media comes up in real life. It's okay to leave those conversations, especially if they're negative.
- Above all, value your one-on-one, real-life connections.
- Separate your self-worth from the number of social media followers you have.
- Learn to ignore the haters.

Write what you have learned or experienced while disconnected.

- _____
- _____
- _____
- _____
- _____
- _____
- _____
- _____
- _____
- _____
- _____
- _____
- _____
- _____

BUILD YOUR PLAYLIST:
SONGS THAT CALM ME DOWN

I listen to these to feel at ease when I'm upset.

Arctic Monkeys "I Wanna Be Yours"

Tom Odell "Another Love"

Melanie Martinez "Bittersweet Tragedy"

Gorillaz "Revolving Doors"

5 Seconds of Summer "San Francisco"

Nothing but Thieves "Graveyard Whistling"

La Roux "Let Me Down Gently"

Write down songs that make you calm, so you can have your own playlist ready when you need it!

PLAYLIST

_____

Created by:

TITLE	ARTIST	ALBUM
+		
+		
+		
+		
+		
+		
+		
+		

◀ ⊙ ▶

MY DOUBLE LIFE

Do you sometimes feel like you lead a double life? Like you're one person in one situation or place, and then a totally different person somewhere else? Write and draw about the two you's.

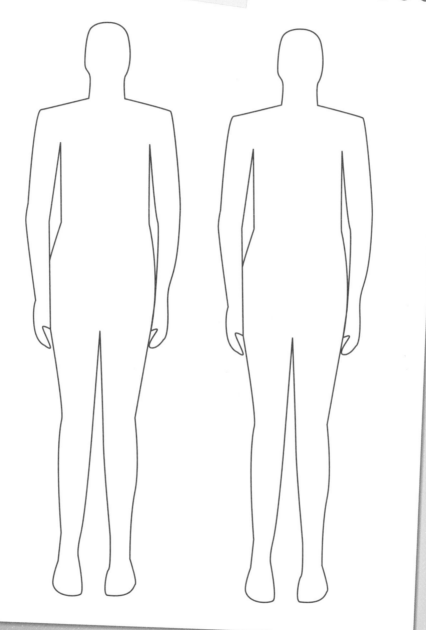

13

@JESSIEPAEGE...MENTAL HEALTH

This topic is really important. Let's talk about it. Read my thoughts and respond.

Jessie Paege ✅ @jessiepaege

mental illness is NOT A CHOICE. people can't just turn it off and on. no one ASKS for it. everyone should respect this.

Jessie Paege ✅ @jessiepaege

the worst thing is when people assume you're lying about mental illness when everyday it makes your life harder and it's so real.

Jessie Paege ✅ @jessiepaege

benefits of mental health days:

- come back more productive
- stress and anxiety can affect physical health
- better relationships with pals

_____ ✅ @_____

_____ ✅ @_____

@YOU

We're in a safe space. So start spilling your real hopes, drives, worries, and fears. In return, I'll do the same for you.

YOU

_____

_____

_____

_____

_____

_____

ME

Things I battle every day: anxiety, insecurity, loneliness, detachment

Grievances: being used, only being looked for when someone wants something from me

Hopes: to keep doing what I love in its purest, most genuine form

Aspirations: a balanced lifestyle, eliminating unhealthy obsessions, living more outside of my own brain and thoughts

ROAST YOURSELF

Making fun of my own insecurities is totally freeing. I wrote this about my YouTube channel.

HEY JESSIE,

YOU SAY THAT YOU'RE A VEGAN, WELL THAT'S DEBATABLE;
YOUR LOVE FOR INDIE MUSIC DOESN'T MAKE YOU THAT
RELATABLE.

WE GET IT, YOU'RE AWKWARD AND INTERNALLY
SCREAMING, BUT YOUR MESSY EDITS WON'T HELP WITH
YOUR VIEWS; YOU MUST BE DREAMING.

STOP ASKING FOR LIKES
THINKING YOU'RE ORIGINAL
AND GO BACK TO
CLUB PENGUIN. YOUR
MATURITY IS CRIMINAL.

YOU COULDN'T EVEN
TAKE CARE OF A DOG IF
YOU TRIED.
SO WHY DO YOUR FANS
CALL YOU "MOM" WITH
PRIDE?

YOUR TURN...

17

@JESSIEPAEGE ... INDEPENDENCE

This topic is near and dear to me. Let's talk about independence.

Jessie Paege ✓ @jessiepaege
things your average teenager doesn't have to think about (but I do!)
- paying rent
- food shopping
- meetings
- laundry (not fun)
- locking the doors and windows

Jessie Paege ✓ @jessiepaege
my life:

staying in > going out
drama in tv shows > drama in my life
independence > dependence
happiness > everything
music >>>

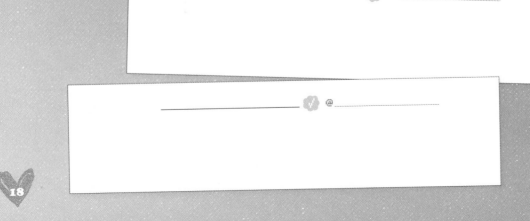
Jessie Paege ✓ @jessiepaege
I just got a ton of pretty little dresses and:

cashier: who are you trying to impress with these? a date?
me: oh no, they're just for me.

_____ ✓ @_____

_____ ✓ @_____

WEIRD THINGS YOU'RE SECRETLY DOING...

I think it's so funny to look back on stuff like this. I secretly plan world domination in my spare time. Relatable!!!

Come on, you know you are secretly doing something weird. So spill.

- _____
- _____
- _____
- _____
- _____
- _____
- _____
- _____
- _____
- _____
- _____
- _____
- _____
- _____
- _____
- _____

OUTER SHELL MIRROR

We all create an outer shell with our clothes, hair, and style. Appearance doesn't make one person more valid than another.

If what you read is true, check the box.

☐ **I WEAR MY HAIR A CERTAIN WAY TO FIT IN.**

☐ **I DON'T DRESS AS WELL AS I WANT TO.**

☐ **I HAVE PARENTS THAT CONTROL MY APPEARANCE TO THE EXTREME.**

☐ **OTHER PEOPLE MAKE COMMENTS THAT MAKE ME FEEL UNCOMFORTABLE ABOUT MY LOOK.**

If you checked any of the boxes, you're not alone. I once felt like the only one at my school who had these issues, but then I grew up and discovered a vast world outside of my little suburban life. Almost everyone struggles with how to present themselves to the outside world.

Now, reflect and tell me what you like about your outer shell.

GOOD VS. BAD

GOOD FRIENDS

- Send memes (lol).
- Have different interests. It gives you more to talk about.
- Appreciate you and help you when they can.
- Are proud of you when you accomplish big things.
- Understand your strange humor and love it.

   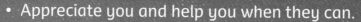

BAD FRIENDS

- Don't like it when you show your true self.
- Talk down to you.
- Don't act with your best interest at heart.
- Let jealousy affect your friendship.
- Make hanging out feel like work because you need to please them.

Write a letter to a good friend. List all the reasons you like them. Share a favorite memory. You don't have to show your friend the letter, but you should!

DEAR _____ ,

_____

_____

_____

_____

_____

_____

_____

_____

_____

_____

_____

_____

_____

_____

_____

_____

_____

_____

 **LOVE,**

_____

WE'RE ALL JUST HUMANS

I love referring to people as "humans." When you do that, it makes all other labels disappear. Write about a memory that always makes you laugh—without using pronouns like he/she/him/her/his/hers.

_____

_____

_____

_____

_____

_____

_____

_____

_____

_____

_____

_____

_____

_____

Isn't it freeing to think of people as just HUMAN?

SUPERHERO ME

Fun fact: I love everything superhero, and I even used to pretend to be a mermaid superhero with my friends. (I know, you're not surprised.) What does your super-self look like? Paste or draw a picture of yourself here. Then make it SUPER!

What's your superhero name? Try combining the color of the shirt you're wearing with your own special talent. Puns are welcome.

WHICH JESSIE ARE YOU?

We all have different sides to ourselves. Which do you identify with today? For each prompt, circle the letter that fits you best.

1. YOUR DAILY DIGITAL LIFE INCLUDES
    a. searching the internet for LOLs
    b. saturating your photos
    c. making playlists
    d. creating dream outfits of dark clothes

2. YOUR CLOSET IS FULL OF
    a. T-shirts with witty sayings on them
    b. rainbow-colored clothes
    c. black skinny jeans
    d. instruments

3. WHEN YOU SEE A CUTE PICTURE, YOU WANT TO
    a. write a funny caption for it
    b. put a pink flower crown filter on it
    c. destroy it
    d. write a song about it

4. YOUR FRIENDS THINK YOU ARE
    a. the funniest person they know
    b. a human highlighter
    c. a little pretentious in your musical tastes
    d. damaging your ears with how loud you play your music

IF YOU CHOSE MOSTLY A, you are Meme Jessie. You're always up to date on the latest memes and collect more memes than friends.

IF YOU CHOSE MOSTLY B, you are Colorful Jessie. You identify with rainbows and don't know how anyone can relate to those "as black as my soul" quotes.

IF YOU CHOSE MOSTLY C, you are Grunge Jessie. Your clothing is in the dark to darker range and your life is full of alternative band worship.

IF YOU CHOSE MOSTLY D, you are Musical Jessie. Music is your life, and you need to be listening to music, learning about music, and creating music at all times.

WINNING INNER BATTLES

When I first started making videos, I became a joke at school. Kids would have group chats to mock my videos. I could have let people making fun of me fuel my insecurity. But I didn't. I dug in. I knew that doing what I loved was more important than what people said about me. I decided to keep making videos. I won my inner battle! It was definitely a first for me.

Think about a time when you had an inner battle. Did you win it? If so, what did you learn? If not, what could you have done differently to win the battle?

_____

_____

_____

_____

_____

_____

_____

_____

_____

_____

_____

_____

_____

_____

@JESSIEPAEGE...INTERNET FRIENDSHIPS

Finding your people—a positive group of friends—is hugely important. Read my thoughts and respond. You don't have to have online friendships to participate.

Jessie Paege @jessiepaege

internet friends are beautiful and VALID

- you don't need to physically see them to be connected
- they survive long distance
- appreciate them

Jessie Paege @jessiepaege

my resolutions:

- meet internet friends
- control my anxiety
- sleep more

- find new music
- create more
- be more positive
- go to concerts

Jessie Paege @jessiepaege

if you feel isolated because of:

- your sexuality
- your appearance
- your mental illness

internet friends can make you feel less lonely

_____ @ _____

BUILD YOUR PLAYLIST:
SONGS THAT MAKE ME SMILE ALWAYS

You know when you're feeling down, and you hear that song that just makes you smile, even though you felt like you might never smile again? Yeah, those songs. Here are some of mine.

Black Kids "I'm Not Gonna Teach Your Boyfriend How to Dance With You"

POWERS "Heavy"

One Direction "Tell Me a Lie" (middle-school Jessie is alive)

The Police "Every Breath You Take"

One Direction "Little Things"

Write down songs that make you smile, so you can have your own playlist ready when you need it!

PLAYLIST

_____

Created by:

TITLE	ARTIST	ALBUM
+		
+		
+		
+		
+		
+		
+		
+		

◄ ▶ ►

_____

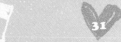

THESE ARE JOKES

Humor is a huge part of my life. I tend to use sarcasm—especially with my brother because he gets it. Try these types of humor on for size:

PUNS

What band does Sherlock Holmes love the most? . . . You guessed it: One Deduction!

What do you call a group of friends who aren't as cool as they seem? Wait for it— clique bait!

Why did the mermaid go on a retreat? To find her life's porpoise.

Write a joke using words that sound like other words.

_____

_____

_____

_____

_____

_____

_____

_____

SARCASM

I literally just fell down the stairs. I'm **SO GRACEFUL!**

My meanest prank was putting a toy under my brother's pillow. I'm an **EVIL GENIUS!**

I have tickets to a **TWENTY ONE PILØTS** concert. I'm not **THAT** excited.

Now you try!

33

AWKWARD

It's probably not news to you that I'm an awkward human. But I'm telling you, you can't even imagine how awkward. Would you believe that I once made a fan account online for my guitar teacher? And he found out it was me! Are you cringing? I still do whenever I think about it. But I wouldn't take back that memory. It reminds me that we're all human, and humans can be flawed.

Write about an awkward experience you've had.
Don't worry, we've all been there.

PRINCESS OBSESSION

Like yours truly, princesses are a lot more than just pretty and pink. They're fierce, and they can teach you a lot if you just pay attention. Now do you know why I'm obsessed?

Snow White

There's strength and power in kindness and a good heart.

Tiana

You can't just sit around waiting for your dreams to come true; you have to get up and make them happen.

Mulan

Never let ANYONE define who you are.

Belle

It's never too late to change your mind about someone.

Ariel

Curiosity leads us to great new opportunities.

Rapunzel

Step out of your comfort zone. There's opportunity waiting out there for you.

Jasmine

There's a great big world out there to explore. So what are you waiting for?

Who are your favorite princesses?

What have you learned from them?

IT'S OKAY TO BE...

AFRAID

Fear is natural. It keeps us away from cliffs where we could fall off and meet our doom. That is a rational fear. But sometimes our brains take fear and apply it to situations that honestly don't require it. I can surely relate.

ADVICE ON TACKLING FEAR

- Remind yourself that you're not the only one with this fear.
- Get to the root of your fear by writing about it. Is it a rational fear, or something you need to move past?
- Challenge your fear. You don't need to face it head-on right away. It took me three years to play guitar in front of people! THREE YEARS!
- Acknowledge how far you've come before getting discouraged.
- Draw a picture of your fear that makes it look less scary and even kind of funny.
- Find a distraction from your fear. Me? I have an emergency playlist.

Write down some fears you have. They look 10x easier to face when they're just words.

- _____
- _____
- _____
- _____
- _____
- _____
- _____
- _____
- _____
- _____

IDENTITY MIRROR

Age, race, and gender are all part of who we are—our identity.

If what you read is true, check the box.

☐ **I HAVE BEEN TOLD I CAN'T DO SOMETHING BECAUSE OF MY GENDER.**

☐ **I HAVE BEEN TOLD I CAN'T DO SOMETHING BECAUSE OF MY AGE.**

☐ **PEOPLE HAVE JUDGED MY INTELLIGENCE BASED ON HOW I LOOK.**

☐ **I HARDLY EVER SEE A HERO ON TV THAT LOOKS LIKE ME.**

So how many boxes did you check?

If you checked any of these boxes, know that you are not alone. Discrimination based on gender, age, race, and appearance happens to people every day. It's important that you learn to recognize when people are putting limits on you. You are a human. You can do anything.

Draw a character that challenges gender norms—like a female race car driver. Or a male school nurse.

JUDGMENT

People judge all the time.

You might see someone loudly making jokes and think they're confident. Or you might see a quiet person and think they're not interesting. If you only know ONE THING about a person, don't think you know EVERYTHING about them.

So what do you do when you're being judged?

Okay, this task is so much fun for me. I write out my weirdest thoughts—real, genuine thoughts. I put them on paper without worrying what people might think. That helps me remember that I'm me, and that's okay.

Write your weirdest thoughts here. No judgment.

_____

_____

_____

_____

_____

_____

_____

_____

_____

Ruby Rose's authenticity shines through— especially with gender identity. I love artists who have powerful voices when it comes to social issues.

Who do you admire for being bold?

GOOD VS. BAD

GOOD ROLE MODELS

- Show you positive things about the world.
- Are genuine in what they do.
- Show you that your goals are achievable.
- Give you a new perspective on life.
- Keep you guessing.

BAD ROLE MODELS

- Focus on the negative.
- Don't care about their supporters.
- Make you question yourself.
- Are in it for the money, clicks, or fame.
- Repeat what's been said before.

Write down what you admire about your role models or favorite creative people. Don't say "she's so pretty" or "he's cute." Appearances are not reasons to respect someone.

INSECURI-T'S

On one of my favorite TV shows, *Glee*, all the characters write their insecurities on T-shirts and then sing. Let's do that. Owning your insecurities make them seem like less of a big deal. Write what makes you uncomfortable on the T-shirts. Singing is optional.

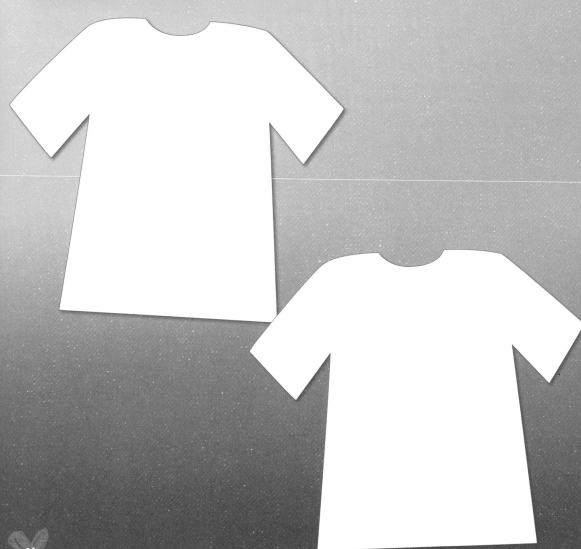

BUILD YOUR PLAYLIST:
SONGS THAT MAKE YOU FEEL LIKE A BOSS

Because. You. Are. A. Boss. Even if you don't feel like one.

Dua Lipa "Be the One"

Marina and the Diamonds "Power & Control"

Sabrina Carpenter "Why"

Troye Sivan "Too Good"

Halsey "Walls Could Talk"

Write down songs that make you feel powerful and in charge.

PLAYLIST

Created by: _____

TITLE	ARTIST	ALBUM
+		
+		
+		
+		
+		
+		
+		
+		

◄ ⊙ ►

VOICE FOR THE VOICELESS

There are a lot of ways to stand up for people, or give voice to the voiceless. Here are a few examples from my life.

CALL IT OUT

Recently, this person started talking trash about my good friend. I bluntly told the person that she was super-rude. That's it. I just stuck up for my friend. Then, right after, the person acted as if nothing happened.

BE AN EXAMPLE

When I was 13 years old, everyone gave out personalized sweatshirts for birthday parties and bar and bat mitzvahs. The day after the party, everyone wore the sweatshirts to school. If you weren't wearing it, it meant you didn't get invited to the party and were not cool. My friends and I agreed to never wear the sweatshirts we got at parties. It was a mean trend, and we did not take part in it.

Have you ever stood up for someone because it was the right thing to do? Write about it here.

_____

_____

_____

_____

_____

_____

_____

_____

_____

_____

_____

_____

_____

_____

_____

_____

_____

_____

_____

INSPIRATIONS

These people helped me become who I am today.

<u>High school teacher</u>: I was insanely shy in school. Teachers were sometimes the only people who listened to me. My high school English teacher once told me that she admired my creativity and how I applied it to all aspects of my life. She enjoyed seeing the fearless outfits and vivid makeup I wore to class. She inspired me to literally be myself.

<u>Friends</u>: Growing up, I was the older sibling. So I had to be the first to do everything. I've always gotten shaken up about new experiences. Now, I have friends that are a year or two older than me. It's like having an amazing friend and an older sibling. They always help me when I'm worried about taking a new step. They inspire me to be bold.

So who inspires you? Write about them here:

@JESSIEPAEGE...KINDNESS

 Jessie Paege ✅ @jessiepaege
it costs $0.00:

- to be kind
- to be tolerant of others
- to listen
- to smile back

 Jessie Paege ✅ @jessiepaege
being nice does not mean:

- people can use you
- people can be mean to you
- people can assume you're not opinionated

 Jessie Paege ✅ @jessiepaege
reminder:

- it costs nothing to compliment
- you're not annoying or belittling yourself by giving compliments
- a compliment can make a person's day

_____ ✅ @ _____

_____ ✅ @ _____

54

MY SCARS

Some scars appear on our skin, but I'm more focused on the emotional battles we all have, and the scars they leave behind. I even have trouble admitting how much my emotional scars hurt.

Draw a picture of one of your emotional scars here. Write about how it makes you feel.

_____

_____

_____

_____

_____

_____

_____

_____

NOW VS. THEN—SCHOOL

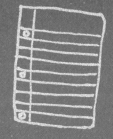

Nothing stays the same and school is no exception.

THEN, I was the queen of the playground when I had a great Pokémon or silly band collection.

NOW, having social media followers is the "cool" thing. WHOA, LOOK AT THOSE DIGITS ON THAT SCREEN!!! Ridiculous.

THEN, kids were totally judging me, and I felt super-shy and insecure.

NOW, I don't care what anyone thinks. I love ME!

THEN, school was _____

_____

NOW, school is _____

_____

THEN, kids at school _____

_____

NOW, kids at school _____

_____

IT'S OKAY TO BE...

AMBITIOUS

Ambitious people can get a bad rap. People call us strivers or think we're full of ourselves. But ambition is about reaching for your goals—small or large. Goals are important, and there's nothing wrong with having a strong desire for success.

ADVICE FOR THE AMBITIOUS

- Set your goals, but don't be afraid to change them if you need to.
- Watch your idols to see what they do to achieve their dreams.
- See the world—let new things, new places, and new people inspire you.
- Don't focus only on money and material things. There's more to life than that—you know this!
- Believe that anything is possible with hard work and determination. I'm proof!

Tell me what your goals are.

PUN O'CLOCK

WHEN YOU GET SOAP IN YOUR MOUTH WHILE SINGING IN THE SHOWER, IT'S A *SOAP OPERA*.

HOW DO I LOOK IN MY PIZZA HALLOWEEN COSTUME? PRETTY *CRUSTY*!

THE LITTLE WHALE DETECTIVE SAID, "*WHALE WHALE WHALE*, WHAT DO WE HAVE HERE?"

"I LOST *CONTROL*," THE GIRL SAID AS SHE SAW HER KEYBOARD HAD A MISSING CONTROL KEY.

THE BAKER'S KITTEN IS *PURE BREAD*. SHE ATE A WHOLE LOAF THIS MORNING.

Now it's your turn. Share your favorite puns.

_____
_____
_____
_____
_____
_____
_____
_____
_____

Draw a cartoon of your favorite pun.

BODY IMAGE MIRROR

Body image is how we think about and judge our bodies.

If what you read is true, check the box.

- ☐ I'VE WORRIED I WAS OVERWEIGHT OR TOO THIN.

- ☐ I'VE FELT UNCOMFORTABLE WITH MY BODY.

- ☐ I'VE BEEN TREATED MEANLY BECAUSE OF MY BODY.

- ☐ I'VE HAD SYMPTOMS OF AN EATING DISORDER.

So how many boxes did you check?

If you did not check a box, wow! You have a great attitude about your body. Help others feel just as comfortable.

If you checked any boxes, pay attention. When it comes to your body, health is important. Everything else is not. Talk to your doctor and make sure you're healthy. Don't let anyone treat you badly.

Now, write how you feel about your body.

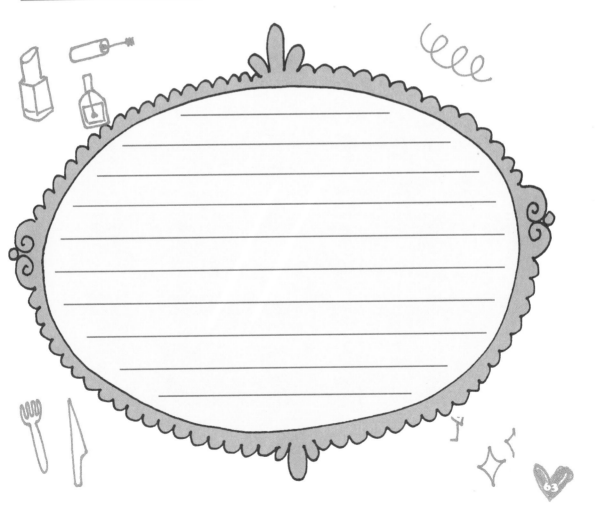

BUILD YOUR PLAYLIST:
NOSTALGIC SONGS

When something is nostalgic, it reminds you of happy memories. Check out these tracks! They always make me feel like I'm wrapped in a musical hug.

Muse "Knights of Cydonia"

OneRepublic "All the Right Moves"

3 Doors Down "Kryptonite"

Florence and the Machine "Dog Days Are Over"

Smash Mouth "All Star"

Owl City "Fireflies"

You know those songs that totally take you back to the good times? Make a playlist of them here!

PLAYLIST

_____

Created by:

TITLE	ARTIST	ALBUM
+		
+		
+		
+		
+		
+		
+		
+		

◄ ⊙ ►

THINGS I LEARNED IN...

I learned something every year in school.

1ST GRADE It's all right to make new friends. You won't offend your old friends.

2ND GRADE You can wear things besides what your parents buy for you.

3RD GRADE Trying out independence can be a beautiful thing.

4TH GRADE Life can be unfair–for EVERYONE.

5TH GRADE Jessie, you need to start doing your homework more.

6TH GRADE Join clubs. It's a liberatingbreak and allows you to have a better relationship with going to school.

7TH GRADE Not all love is created equal.

8TH GRADE Reputation isn't everything.

9TH GRADE Jessie, you failed your nutrition test and can't run a mile. WORK ON THAT.

10TH GRADE Independence is incredible.

11TH GRADE If you're unhappy, you need to do something about it.

12TH GRADE There's social life, work, and school. You can't have all three. Your social life helps keep you sane.

So, what have you learned in school? Fill in this page as you complete each grade.

1ST GRADE

2ND GRADE

3RD GRADE

4TH GRADE
5TH GRADE

6TH GRADE

7TH GRADE
8TH GRADE
9TH GRADE

10TH GRADE
11TH GRADE

12TH GRADE

67

IT'S OKAY TO BE...

OPINIONATED

As you can probably tell, I have opinions. I share my opinions all the time. Don't let anyone tell you that you shouldn't have opinions. Share them. Talk about them. Be open to new ones.

ADVICE ON SHARING OPINIONS

- I know you believe in things and people...so stand up for them!
- Think about how your words might affect the person you're saying them to.
- Be intentional with your words. Are you giving your opinion, or passing judgment?
- Know when to stop. If you see someone else getting upset, it's probably time to take a breather.
- Don't let your personal style hurt your case. I'm all about sarcasm, but I speak from the heart when it's important.

What are you most opinionated about?

- _____
- _____
- _____
- _____
- _____
- _____
- _____
- _____
- _____
- _____

BUILD YOUR PLAYLIST:
SONGS THAT BRING ME COMFORT

Check out these tracks! They always make me feel like I'm wrapped in a musical hug.

Fleetwood Mac "Albatross"

(Thanks, Dad!)

My Morning Jacket "Gideon"

Embrace "Why"

Karen O & Ezra Koenig

"The Moon Song"

Youth Lagoon "17"

What's your comfort playlist? Share the songs here.

PLAYLIST

_____

Created by:

TITLE	ARTIST	ALBUM
+		
+		
+		
+		
+		
+		
+		
+		

◄ ⊳ ►

71

MENTAL HEALTH BREAK

Our mental health is just as important as our physical health. So if you need to take a break to feel better, take it! Just make sure to plan your break the right way.

Here's my plan:

EAT

Comfort food. I like to freeze hot chocolate and then have it as chocolate ice cream.

Vegan mac and cheese

Vegan peppermint mocha

Vegan cookie dough

WATCH/LISTEN TO

Feel-good films like The Goonies, The Karate Kid, Mulan

Comedy throwbacks like Saved by the Bell, iCarly, Drake & Josh

TWENTY ØNE PILØTS-ALWAYS!

STAY AWAY FROM

Social media

Notifications

Toxic people

EAT

_____
_____
_____
_____
_____

WATCH/LISTEN TO

_____
_____
_____
_____
_____

STAY AWAY FROM

_____
_____
_____

RELATIONSHIPS WITH FOOD

I often see people showing off how much or how little they eat. This happens A LOT on social media. But an unhealthy relationship with food is a big sign that something is going on with your mental health. It's not a joke. It's not cute. It's something to address.

These things don't even seem like a big deal, but they're signs of an unhealthy relationship with food:

- Binging on ice cream whenever you're upset.
- Not eating when you're anxious.

Please be aware, take it seriously, and watch out for your friends. If you or they need real help, reach out to an adult you can trust, like your guidance counselor or family doctor.

Draw a picture that shows your relationship with food.

Note any signs of unhealthy food relationships here. Being aware is the first step.

@JESSIEPAEGE...EQUALITY

All people are equal, including you. Discuss!
Read my thoughts and respond.

 Jessie Paege ✓ @jessiepaege
we should stop invalidating humans because of

- their appearance
- their # of followers
- the amount of money they have
- their clothes

 Jessie Paege ✓ @jessiepaege
who says:

- boys can't have mermaid dolls
- girls can't play sports with boys
- boys can't enjoy cooking
- girls can't play video games

 Jessie Paege ✓ @jessiepaege
people should not be ignored/disregarded because of:

- hair color
- grades
- style
- race
- sexuality
- age

_____ ✓ @_____

_____ ✓ @_____

76

HOW STRONG IS YOUR MEME GAME?

THINGS TO DO WHEN YOU'RE STUCK IN YOUR OWN MIND

Feeling stuck? There's a lot of ways to keep your creativity flowing. Try some of these!

TAKE UP A NEW INSTRUMENT

WRITE DOWN YOUR DREAMS AND READ THEM AND GET EMOTIONAL

GO OUTSIDE AND PAY ATTENTION TO ALL THE SOUNDS AND SMELLS AROUND YOU

GET OUT YOUR BLOCKS OR LEGOS AND BUILD SOMETHING

REREAD A PART OF YOUR FAVORITE BOOK

THINK ABOUT GREAT MEMORIES YOU'VE HAD

NOW VS. THEN—TRENDS

Have trends changed since you were a little kid? I think so!

THEN, I used to look up Harry Potter spells and cast them on my brother when he wasn't looking. (I still do this. Sorry, Matt.)

NOW, I use a fidget spinner while listening to my favorite bands, and it haunts me.

THEN, I counted my Club Penguin friends like pennies in a piggy bank.

NOW, I make my voice heard on social media.

THEN, everyone was _____

_____

NOW, everyone is _____

_____

THEN, my friends _____

_____

NOW, my friends _____

_____

ECSTATIC

What's wrong with being ecstatic—being filled with overwhelming happiness? NOTHING! But you know, there will always be some people who are going to try to throw shade on your happiness. Don't pay attention to the haters.

LITERALLY WHAT TO DO NOW

- Write a letter to yourself about this moment.
- Haven't jumped around much lately? Now's your chance.
- Take a happy selfie. Leave out the filters. Be your true self.
- Give your happiness a social media shout-out.
- Make something beautiful. An outfit, a drawing, anything.
- Send a friend a message to make them feel happy. It's one of my favorite things to do.

What makes you ecstatic?

- _____
- _____
- _____
- _____
- _____
- _____
- _____
- _____
- _____
- _____
- _____
- _____
- _____

WHO YOU LOVE

I want to talk straight to you about human sexuality. It is a natural part of our lives that grows with us. At some point, every human will be attracted to another human. Some girls will be attracted to boys, and vice versa. Some girls will be attracted to other girls, and some boys to other boys.

People are so obsessed with who's dating who, but the thing is, it doesn't really matter. You love who you love, and you shouldn't be judged for it. Remember that—not just for yourself, but for your friends, your family, and everyone.

And the most important relationship is the one you have with yourself. Know yourself. Love and accept every part of you. Then you can love and accept the people around you too.

LABELS

Labels can be a beautiful thing when you choose them yourself. They allow you to find a community and discover your identity. They can also be used against you. Use this space to choose positive labels for yourself.

HELLO, I'M . . .

HELLO, I'M . . .

HELLO, I'M . . .

HELLO, I'M . . .

HELLO, I'M . . .

Look back at this page after a few years. It'll fascinate you.

SOCIAL MEDIA DO'S AND DON'TS

Social media can be a tool for good or bad. If you're going to use it, do it right.

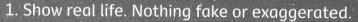

DO

1. Show real life. Nothing fake or exaggerated.
2. Post photos other than selfies. Post what you see in the world.
3. Represent your own style.
4. Follow accounts that inspire you.
5. Like posts because you like them, not for other reasons.

DON'T

1. Shade people. It's petty. Just be nice.
2. Respond to haters. It's not worth your time.
3. Post videos of things that don't belong to you.
4. Care about looking good in photos. I literally never think about that.
5. RELY ON PICTURES GOING AWAY. NOTHING IS COMPLETELY GONE ONCE IT IS POSTED. Post like it's GOING TO BE THERE FOR ALL TIME.

Do you use social media well? Write some promises to yourself. What will you do and not do on social media?

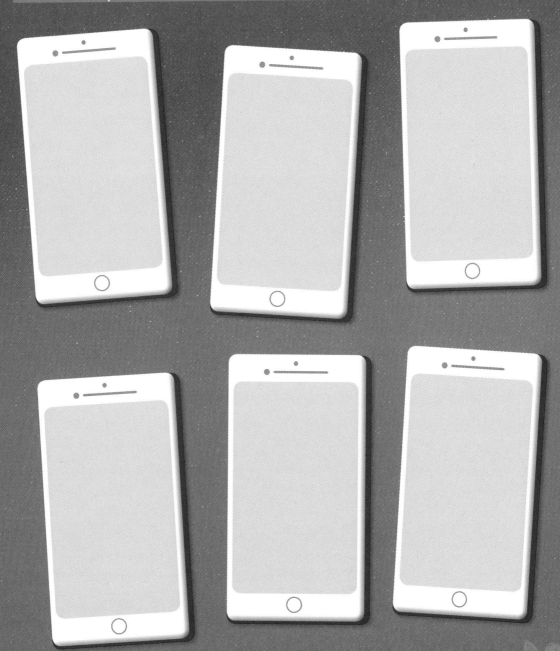

WHICH OBJECT IN JESSIE'S APARTMENT ARE YOU?

People are not objects, okay? But let's see what this quiz says about you.

1. YOUR FAVORITE COLOR IS
a. electric blue
b. stainless steel
c. don't make me choose!
d. wood grain

2. YOU'RE KNOWN FOR ASKING
a. "Can you turn up the volume on my amp?"
b. "Can you pick me up some cashew butter?"
c. "Are you going to the pride parade next weekend?"
d. "Did you see this kitten meme?"

3. ON YOUR READING LIST
a. guitar tabs
b. cookbooks
c. so many biographies
d. comic books

4. YOUR FAVORITE ACCESSORY IS
a. a pair of guitar pick earrings
b. your strawberry knit hat
c. your multicolored striped scarf
d. your emoji backpack

IF YOU CHOSE MOSTLY A, you are Jessie's electric guitar. You're bold and unique. You can sometimes be a little loud, but you ALWAYS rock!

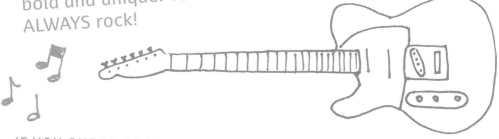

IF YOU CHOSE MOSTLY B, you are Jessie's refrigerator. You're a vegan foodie. You know where to get the best coconut milk ice cream and eggless brownies.

IF YOU CHOSE MOSTLY C, you are Jessie's giant rainbow on her wall. You embrace differences, and you're a warrior for social justice issues.

IF YOU CHOSE MOSTLY D, you are Jessie's ukelele. You're fun and entertaining. You're low maintenance and don't sweat over the details; you just want life to be a simple, pretty tune.

NOW VS. THEN—MUSIC

Music is always changing. But then again, it always comes back around again.

THEN, I listened to music and pretended to be a pop star all the time. I was told I looked like Miley Cyrus when I was little so I—in a low-key fashion—wanted to be her.

NOW, I view music as a form of art and my respect for it and those who create it grows every day.

THEN, I played the same five songs over and over again—the High School Musical soundtrack is a classic.

NOW, I am always looking for new songs to listen to. I'm always excited for a new TWENTY ØNE PILØTS song!

THEN, music was _____

_____

NOW, music is _____

_____

THEN, I liked music that _____

_____

NOW, I like music that _____

_____

ANXIOUS?

Feeling anxious is like feeling nervous, but so much worse. I get anxiety when there's attention on me. I can't even play a video game in front of my brother. But ignoring anxiety won't make it go away. These are tips and advice that helped me.

ANXIOUS IN SCHOOL:
- Make a playlist . . . try the calm playlist on page 10.
- Tell someone how you feel.

ANXIOUS WITH FRIENDS:
- Lean on close friends if you have them.
- Leave groups that treat you badly.
- Practice. I used to be anxious about MAKING friends. It took a while, but I just kept trying until I got comfortable.

ANXIOUS ABOUT THE FUTURE:
- Remember this: No one knows how their future will unfold.
- Yes, it's scary not knowing what will happen to you. It's okay to notice that.
- Worrying and constantly stressing about it won't make anything better. Talk about it!

BREATHE

DREAM

PEACE

LOVE

FRIENDSHIP

MUSIC

@JESSIEPAEGE...LOVE

This topic is everything. Read my thoughts and respond.

Jessie Paege ✔ @jessiepaege
I love texting people I know little paragraphs telling them how cool they are and how much I appreciate them.
I'm soft ok?

Jessie Paege ✔ @jessiepaege
I was next to a cute old gay couple on my flight and they were holding hands like "do you mind?" and I was like "no. no one should."

Jessie Paege ✔ @jessiepaege
reminder:

- your body keeps u alive: appreciate that and give it what it needs
- if someone only loves u for your body then drop them

_____ ✔ @_____

_____ ✔ @_____

_____ ✔ @_____

POINTS OF VIEW

My brother Matt is my favorite person on the planet, but we don't always see things the same way. We experience moments differently. Here's how we both describe the same memories.

SCHOOL

MATT: I'd say "hi," and Jessie wouldn't respond. In school, everyone called me Jessie's brother. I'd go up to Jessie in study hall, and she'd walk away, and not come back.

JESSIE: I was awkward and Matt was outgoing. I would stick to my few close friends. Matt would say "hi," and I'd be too shy to yell a "hello" back.

BIRTHDAY

MATT: I was the only guy at Jessie's birthday party, and I had to dress up as a fairy. I was a monarch butterfly, but it just looked really stupid.

JESSIE: Matt was such a supportive brother. He even dressed up as a fairy at my birthday party and challenged his masculinity. What a guy.

Write about a memory you share with someone else. Then, ask them to describe the same memory. The difference in the stories will fascinate you!

_____

_____

_____

_____

_____

SELF-APPRECIATION TIME

Do you love yourself? I mean, do you really take time to love yourself? It's soooo easy to forget to do that. Use this page to give yourself some love.

Spend five minutes just taking deep breaths.

On a piece of paper, write down 10 words that describe your positive qualities. Fold it up and keep it so you can read it whenever you're feeling down about yourself.

Text 4 people a cute little paragraph about how you appreciate them. Then write one for yourself.

INCREDIBLE YOU

Go on, tell me what's great about you. I'm waiting....

- _____
- _____
- _____
- _____
- _____
- _____
- _____
- _____
- _____
- _____
- _____
- _____
- _____
- _____
- _____
- _____
- _____
- _____
- _____
- _____

WHY I LOVE YOUTUBERS!

My career started on YouTube, and I grew up watching YouTubers. I even went to the Tyler Oakley tour. While I was in line, I became best friends with these girls because they had other YouTubers I liked on their phone cases. Growing up with these powerful voices definitely has inspired me and continues to inspire me.

YouTubers rock because they are:
- Multitalented
- Friendly!
- Hardworking
- Appreciative
- Independent, and write their own scripts
- Open to topics that TV networks won't touch
- Genuine—I feel much more connected to YouTubers than people on TV

Who are some YouTubers or creators you love?

_____

_____

_____

_____

_____

What would your YouTube channel be like? Write about it.

CHANNEL NAME _____

HOST _____

LOCATION, LOCATION, LOCATION _____

_____

TYPES OF VIDEOS _____

_____

_____

TOPICS _____

_____

_____

GUESTS AND COLLABORATORS _____

_____

_____

IT'S OKAY TO BE...

I mean literally you, not some fake persona or who you think you should be. Be yourself and you'll find what makes you happy.

Let's review!

WHEN I FIRST STARTED THE BOOK, I FELT _____
_____ ABOUT MYSELF.

NOW I FEEL _____ .

THREE PIECES OF ADVICE I'M GOING TO USE IN MY LIFE...

1. _____
2. _____
3. _____

A letter to future you:

DEAR _____ ,

_____
_____
_____
_____
_____
_____
_____
_____
_____
_____
_____
_____
_____
_____
_____

LOVE,

_____

BEYOND THE BOOK

Now that we've thought about the way we see ourselves and the world...what are we going to do differently?

I'M ON A MAJOR MISSION TO find different ways to express myself creatively. I want to keep creating new video content, but I want to push myself even further.

ASPIRATIONS

- Have a clothing or makeup line (style is a huge part of myself and my brand)
- Build out a brand from my Internet presence
- Become a better public speaker (still working on it)
- Gain confidence

I'M ON A MAJOR MISSION TO _____

_____

_____

_____

ASPIRATIONS

- _____
- _____
- _____
- _____
- _____
- _____

SHOUT-OUTS

I am inspired by so many people. I am so thankful for them.
Let's shout out the people who light up our lives.

Jordan Doww – One of the funniest and most real guys I know. He's also too genuine and kind for this world.

Hayley Williams – One of the most pure and sweet humans. She works hard for everything she gets and takes nothing for granted.

JenerationDIY – She's insanely creative and hardworking AND nice. I love it.

THE VOICE BEYOND THE MADNESS

So who is the human who took you on this journey?

I am the host of a lifestyle, comedy, and advice YouTube channel, @JessiePaege. There, I discuss topics like the ones in this book and so much more. I currently live in Los Angeles, California, with my dog. This is my first book.

JESSIE PAEGE FAST FACTS

BIRTHDAY: March 12

ZODIAC SIGN: Pisces

HEIGHT: 5' 11"

FAVORITE SUBJECTS: English and math

WORST SUBJECTS: gym

THINGS I MISS: Spending time with my brother, Matt. He's a meme on his weekends.

FAVORITE SNACK: Hot cocoa (FROZEN OMG)

THE LOOKS

This was when the pink trend started. Do I look worried about Fashion Week? LOL, no.

This is my brother and I pretending we like each other.

Bring back the green hair?